A Unicorn's Wish

by
Lori Chown

The Magical World of Utopia

A Unicorn's Wish

By

Lori Chown

Pictures and Illustrations by:

Lori Chown

Published by:

Utopian Dreams Gifts

Table of Contents

Make the world more Utopian!

Lori Chau

Lucy sat listening to the
fountain bubbling.
The clouds in the sky were
looking rather troubling.

Rain and lightning
were all about.
The park was empty,
no people were out.

2

But then the clouds cleared
and a beautiful rainbow

soon appeared.

Beyond the rainbow, magic was real,
the creatures you'd find there
were very surreal.

Lucy was told that if she flew
with all of her might she could
get through to the other side.

So Lucy flew towards the rainbow
as fast as she could,
still not sure
if it would do any good.

When Lucy entered the rainbow,
fireworks exploded before her eyes.
Beautiful colors were
ablaze in the sky.

Lucy couldn't believe her eyes.
Millions of stars sparkled in the sky.
The story of Utopia was true!
To get there Lucy just flew.

In front of Lucy stood a beautiful unicorn.
On its head was a magical horn.
"Hello there. I'm Amber," the unicorn
said, as she slowly bowed her head.

"Hi Amber," Lucy said in shock
as she landed by a nearby
heart-shaped rock.

"Welcome to Utopia, a world
that is hard for some to believe.
Utopia is so beautiful
it is hard to conceive."

1

"But because you believed
you were able to get through.
You have the gift of Utopia
right inside of you."

"Utopia is a world
where wishes come true,
and now that you are here
we have a favor to ask of you."

"If you can help us
it would mean a lot.
It would mean the magic on Earth
would not be forgot."

16

"How can I help?
I'm just a dragonfly.
Whatever it is
I'll give it a try."

"It is getting harder and harder
for people to believe.
Something as beautiful as Utopia
is hard for them to conceive."

18

"Here is a basket full of wishes to take back with you. This basket will let others' wishes come true."

1

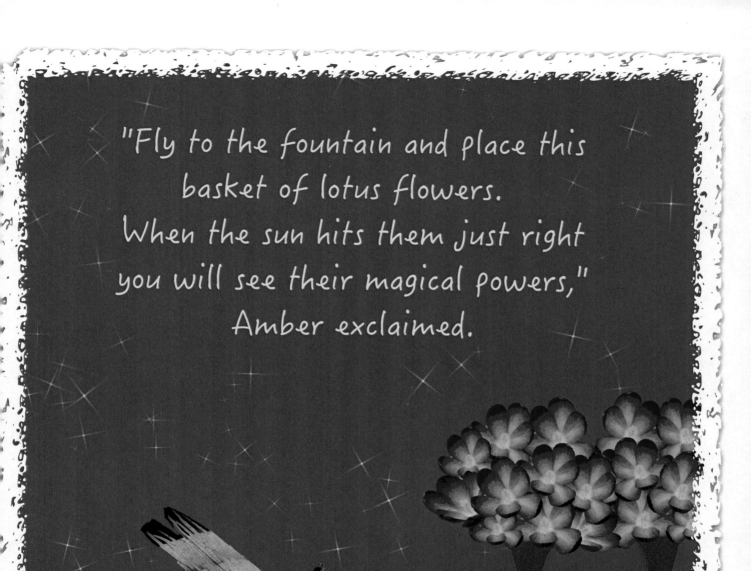

"Fly to the fountain and place this
basket of lotus flowers.
When the sun hits them just right
you will see their magical powers,"
Amber exclaimed.

"I can do that
and I'd be happy to.
Especially if it means
others' wishes will come true."

"Thank you my friend,
for making sure the
magic does not end."

"You are welcome Amber.
Utopia is so beautiful
I want others to see
how beautiful our world can be."

Lucy flew through the rainbow as fast as she could, carrying the flowers that she said she would.

The sky exploded
with fireworks,
looking like a piece of artwork.

The park was quiet,
there was no one in sight.
It looked so peaceful
in the new morning light.

Lucy placed the lotus flowers
in the fountain, just right.
When the sun smiled at them,
they sparkled –
Oh, what an amazing sight!

28

The magic of Utopia is true.
If you look closely,
you'll find little pieces in you!

About Utopian Dreams

We hope you enjoyed *Utopian Dreams'*
A Unicorn's Wish
Please take a moment to review
this book on Amazon.com
Utopian Dreams' inspirational picture books are designed to help
you and your child find a little more
Faith, Hope, and Inspiration.

Utopian Dreams Books presents a series of children's picture books that help build our *Utopianisms*. *Utopianisms* are values that help make the world a little more utopian. Values such as faith, hope, inspiration, love, honesty, compassion, courage, forgiveness, responsibility, confidence, environmentalism, and much more. We hope our stories help you and your child find a little more faith, hope & inspiration. Each book focuses on and lists the key utopianism's that are infused into our story.

Learn more about *Utopian Dreams* at:
http://utopiandreamsgifts.webs.com
https://www.etsy.com/shop/UtopianDreamsGifts
https://www.facebook.com/Utopiandreamsgifts
http://www.amazon.com/Lori-Chown/

Utopian Dreams ~ The Miracle Series

The Miracle Series

The Miracle Series is the first series of Utopian Dreams Books. This series brings to life the everyday miracles that surrounds us, reminding us to always believe.

I See A Miracle

I See A Miracle is the first picture book in the Miracle Series. The world around us is filled with miracles, some great and some small.   I See a Miracle is a beautifully illustrated book that brings these miracles to life, while also encouraging readers to remember and appreciate everyday miracles. Share your faith with your children and help them to see God's love, and how it is infused into every little thing in the world around us.

Utopianism - Faith, Environmentalism, Confidence

Beautiful Baby

Beautiful Baby is part of The Miracle Series. It takes the heartwarming poem Twinkle Twinkle Little Star and creates a bed time story to share with your newborn. This heartwarming poem reminds us what a miracle our little ones are.

Utopianism - Love, Faith, Confidence

Animal ABC's, All of God's Creatures

Animal ABC's is part of the Miracle Series. It teaches little ones the alphabet, while reminding them that we are all God's creatures, and each of us is a miracle. All God's creatures live together on Earth, each of us with value, each of us have worth.

Utopianism - Environmentalism, Compassion, Confidence, Faith

Utopian Dreams ~ The Magical World of Utopia

The Magical World of Utopia

The Magical World of Utopia is the second series of Utopian Dreams Books. This is a heartwarming series that explores the mystical world and creatures of Utopia. Utopia is a beautiful world where unicorns and magic come to life. While Utopia is a make-believe world, these stories will remind you to always believe. Each story takes you on a different adventure, while sharing a little utopianism.

A Unicorn's Wish

A Unicorn's Wish is the first in a series of inspirational children's books about Utopia. The World of Utopia is a world where unicorns and magic are very real. Join Lucy, the dragonfly, as she discovers the Magical World of Utopia and see how Lucy helps bring a little magic from Utopia back to our world.

Utopianism - Courage, Belief, Confidence

The Lost Unicorn

Amber, our magical unicorn from A Unicorn's Wish, finds herself lost and scared in our world. Join Amber and Lucy as they discover the way home isn't as easy as they had thought it would be.

Utopianism - Compassion, Belief, Faith

Fly With Me

Join our dragonfly, Lucy, as she discovers the joy of friendship. Fly With Me takes your child on a journey with two non-traditional friends, a dragonfly and a caterpillar. The story of these friends will teach your child about bullying, friendship, self-value and acceptance.

Utopianism - Acceptance, Self-confidence

40891364R00022

Made in the USA
San Bernardino, CA
31 October 2016